EYES OF THE EAGLE

This collection of poems, written by ONE of America's soldiers, is dedicated to ALL of America's soldiers--past, present, and future. May we never forget the sacrifices these men and women made, and will continue to make, to keep our country safe.

MAJ (Retired) Edwin C. Livingston
Infantry, Special Forces
Angry Skipper

This collection of material is copyrighted © 2008 by Edwin C. Livingston – all rights reserved.
ISBN: 978-0-6152-2381-0

TABLE OF CONTENTS

	PAGE
The Eagle Never Even Cried	1
Bastard Son	2
Winds of Terror	3
Satan's Dome	4
Power of the Thorn	5
I Remember When You Fell	6
Course of the Eagle	7
A Silent Trumpet Blows	8
The Warrior	9
Last War	10
Where Flows the Angry Waters	11
Soldier	12
Fires of Hell	13
Thanks	14
Queen of Battle	15
The Ship	16
The Great American Way	17
Dead Survivors	18
One Black Rose	19
Flight 341	20
Angels on the Battlefield	21
You Made Me What I'm Not Today	22
The Silver Star	23
A Valley Called Ia Drang	24
The Dark Side of Now	25
Children of Stone	26
The Script's Final Page	27
That One Final Day	28
Oh Withered Rose	29
Hatred in Friendly Skies	30
September 11th, Two Thousand and One	31
Heroes	32

	PAGE
Osama Bin Laden	33
Those Harbor Lights	34
Beyond Shadows of Gray	35
Final Hour	36
No One Should Have to Walk This Earth Alone	37
We Fought Too	38

(and on the lighter side)

Bubba Joe's Gone a Huntin'	41

Note: Patriotic symbols courtesy of www.patrioticon.org

THE EAGLE NEVER EVEN CRIED

The unforgiving scent of Death
Accents the mournful Bugler's call;
With trembling hands, I clench my fists
As I face the long Black Wall.

Our flag lies limp in the blowing wind
Grass never grows upon the mound;
A sentry stalks the horrid field
Where blood has soaked the ground.

My friends were slain where vultures prey
Yes... over fifty thousand died;
Yet I was never allowed to question why
And the Eagle never even cried.

No... the Eagle never cried.

In a foreign field where battles raged
I see now as a forgotten shrine;
Where live streams shall never flow free again
And the sun shall never shine.

Salt-laced rain drips down my face
God, how it burns my aging eyes;
While the bitter wind penetrates my skin
I can hear those ghostly cries.

Winds of terror, please go away
God knows how hard I've tried;
To say goodbye to all who fell
And the Eagle ever even cried.

No... the Eagle never cried.

BASTARD SON

The Eagle would soar, its might wings spread
A sentry of power on the fields where we bled;
There's nothing but evil in a war that's undone
I've been there, Sir, I'm your Bastard Son.

From the trenches of doom, their bodies would rot
Sacrifices of the brave, only too soon forgot;
Above half-mast, our flag should never be flown
In respect to the honor of the fallen we've known.

Through the winds of sorrow, in the grasp of pain
The horizon hoards an everlasting rain;
On death-scented fields, the number would mount
Names inscribed in black granite, too numerous to count.

Some view the flag as a crutch, not a symbol of pride
As it was in battle, for those who had died;
She still waves in the wind with particular flair
In search of respect from those who still care.

The scream of the Eagle, not nearly so loud
That once humbled the coward and honored the proud;
Its image is fading, like the spirit we once won
I've been there, Sir, I'm your Bastard Son.

WINDS OF TERROR

Winds of Terror, your mark is known
No gentle breezes where you have blown;
You hurl like bullets, uprooted trees
A form of nature not here to please.

The soldier lives in constant fright
You've drained him of his will to fight;
Victory could never again be attained
All battlefields have been sustained.

Just inches from glory, possibly fame
Was the sentry posted when the end finally came;
The blood-red fires absorbed all the air
The strong grew weak and didn't seem to care.

Sergeants were angered but they couldn't yell
As they were led one by one through the Corridors of Hell;
Humanity has been consumed by the gutters of greed
To reap only the fruits of its own poison seed.

Winds of Terror, Winds of Pain
You shall never have to blow again;
No living soul will again be heard
Humanity shall soon become only a word.

SATAN'S DOME

A summer breeze seeps through the southern pines
With the mournful sound of those lonesome times;
The rushing waters from an unruly stream
Awakens me from that frightening dream.

My friends were there in battle dress
As the days passed on, there were less and less;
I remember their stories of way back home
Before being sent off to Satan's Dome.

They were all just children, young and old
Expendable pawns my country sold;
The fields of fire from the Devil's breath
Engulfed my friends to a certain death.

They marched us there in an endless file
Demeaning our purpose each blood-smeared mile;
Bags for the fallen were dropped from the air
Destined to where maybe someone would care.

I've felt the breeze and smelled the pine
And I've soaked my brain with the two-bit wine;
There are no more fields where the gallant roam
I dream now only of Satan's Dome.

POWER OF THE THORN

God forgives those who would crumple a rose
And fail to plant a new seed;
No life is just without faith and trust
Of the Lord's presence in one's time of need.

In a pasture of dreams, old memories it seems
Will fade in the passing of years;
There can be no relief if there is no belief
That faith overcomes all fears.

From the thorn there is pain, thus, violence shall reign
Where man's blood seeps through the ground;
Each day is undone, no battle ever won
When no reason for hatred is found

Power of the thorn, bears the rose reborn
New life in a shadow of shame;
Though its bud may be weak, strength it shall seek
In the valley where the lost once came.

God forgives those who would crumple a rose
Should he acknowledge the burden of sin;
In a choir of song, there is forgiveness of wrong
Within the heart where feelings begin.

I REMEMBER WHEN YOU FELL

I remember when you fell, my friend
At dusk under a blood-red sky;
The ugly roar from guns afar
Told us someone had to die.

It could have been me you know
I'll wonder why my whole life through;
Maybe God just liked you best
That's why I stayed instead of you.

Yes, I saw you when you fell, my friend
I remember you oh so well;
We fought our way down the path of Glory
That led through the Gates of Hell.

Right or wrong, time passes on
Leaving scars that shall never heal;
Many considered it a war of make believe
You and I found it very, very real.

I remember when you fell, my friend
In the heat of the Asian sun;
If only you and I could have had the courage
To turn our backs and run.

COURSE OF THE EAGLE

The decay of presence shall make life non-absolute
Our existence shall be a portrayal of stone;
Laughter shall be echoed only through the sounds of nature
As the Eagle soars closer to the ground.

The magnificence of progression shall no longer be measured
Time, progress, and future shall be stricken from vocabulary;
The surgeon dies first, to be followed by the lawyer
Should the Eagle shorten its flight.

Mascara shall no longer add beauty to the eyes
As the eye will hollow from hunger and depict sadness;
All shall be crippled by emotion beyond all hope
Should the Eagle fly off course.

The alien shall be ourselves, especially within ourselves
As we meet again and again, it shall always be as strangers;
Yesterday, today, and tomorrow can never again be
Should the Eagle crash.

A SILENT TRUMPET BLOWS

Glory fields again shall mass our sons
Arming them with killing guns;
Angry signals from blood-red skies
Dictate the course the eagle flies.

Their rigid stance and sightless glare
Instills an emptiness in the stagnate air;
Tense bodies tremble with the Sergeant's yell
As their future ensures an impending hell.

Weep, mothers, weep, as your sons go away
Bid a mournful farewell, kiss them you may;
A journey so doomed, it's a mother who knows
The rhythm of death, as a silent trumpet blows.

Youthful expressions so torn from anger and fear
Stripped of all feelings, deprived of a tear;
Burdens of the differences, thrust in their face
The power of power, soon lost beyond trace.

As darkness engulfs the glory field
Sons of war thrust through the deadly shield;
Agonizing sounds of screams from pain
Are drowned out by the falling rain.

Weep, mothers, weep, you're now a Gold Star
Your sons are at peace, wherever they are;
They fell without glory, oh how gallant were those
Death their reward, as a silent trumpet blows.

THE WARRIOR

The warrior has fallen
His legacy shall follow;
Was he our guardian from fear
Or did he man the gallows?

I heard him cry triumphantly
A blood-stained sword at his side;
Cannons barely heard above the sound
When the orphaned child cried.

Should we form a parade of Glory
In honor of his worldly deed?
Or let him rot above the ground
To symbolize our greed.

No, we must bury him with honor
At least to hide our shame;
Place a marker upon his grave
It need not bear a name.

The last warrior has fallen
The trumpeter's eyes are filled with tears;
He will play his trumpet one last time
To the sound the warrior fears.

LAST WAR

I hear the muffled echo of the thundering guns
While brother faces brother again;
Total devastation of all mankind
Can only assure a win.

Man cannot be at peace with man
It just never was meant to be;
The blame is placed where it doesn't belong
Filling life full of uncertainty.

Babies are taught hatred in various forms
From infancy to their puberty line;
Their life then forms only tangible values
While the life line they draw is so fine.

All must face this battle call
This war will finally end all hate;
Guns will silence only when the last one falls
And Peter locks the gate.

Their blood trickles all around me
I feel the thud of the fallen brave;
But I found peace so long ago
Lying here in my grave.

WHERE FLOWS THE ANGRY WATERS

Where flows the angry waters
A breeze has never blown;
Barren banks conceal the path
Of all of life's unknown.

I've bathed in blood where cannons roar
Sounds of death so often heard;
I am the witness of those who fell
But I uttered not a word.

Where flows the angry waters
Fierce currents drug me down;
I gasped for breath, reached for life
Existence was all I found.

There's an innocence within my heart
While evil lures my mind;
I screamed for guidance silently
In this life very much unkind.

Where flows the angry waters
Meandering down a fruitless path;
My presence is noted with uncertainty
As I'm consumed in the basin of wrath.

SOLDIER

In the cries of battle, a warrior's born
Ordered to preserve his country's will;
Becomes an embittered man at seventeen
He has learned to love to kill.

He'll never kneel in prayer again
And apologize, he will not;
He has mastered war and claimed his victories
While wandering through human rot.

He faces the sky and curses God
For the hell and tragedies he has faced;
The once held love for his fellow man
With hatred that loves replaced.

The day then comes that ends the war
Through negotiated peace;
But the soldier fails to comprehend
Why killing his fellow man must cease.

Soldier, Soldier, come back home
Leave your weapon far behind;
Your country thanks you graciously
But as to your needs, they'll all be blind.

FIRES OF HELL

From the streets of hope to the valley of death
We fought the fierce fires of Satan's breath;
There's no one to praise, no one to mourn
In every death, there are three more born.

Mother, oh mother, give me your son
I shall feed him, clothe him, give him a gun;
He will follow me across the fields of fate
As we pierce the walls of fear and hate.

I still hear the cries, I hear the screams
As we marched through the fields of shattered dreams;
For all that would fall, a prayer was then said
To either comfort the living or honor the dead.

Mother, dear mother, I have your son
He'll soldier away until his life is done;
He left his Bible, far to the rear
Feeling imminent death, he must conquer his fear.

His war is now over, the battle's been lost
Unknown to so many the suffering it cost;
The fires of Satan scorch the grounds where they fell
As I continue my journey through the fires of hell.

THANKS

As the flames diminish from the horrors of war
The numbers become fewer in count;
Those Far Eastern fields, so distant from home
Where the stenches of death still mount.

Forgotten were many, remembered were few
Are those for whom the call was heard;
Denied all truths, painfully burdened with lies
All lived void of the unspoken word.

They are seen, though not heard, bearing no resemblance
To the breed of the present day ranks;
There is no question of a nation's debt unpaid
That could be satisfied with the showing of thanks.

Like eternal presence of the midnight sun
It's there, though not in heavenly view;
Fading ranks go unnoticed of a lost generation
The thankless, the faceless, the few.

Charred remains of a memory that shall linger forever
As darkness brings silence to those;
The unheralded ones, to most, the unknown
In time, shall die, like an un-watered rose.

QUEEN OF BATTLE

I am the son of the Queen of Battle
Born at the age of seventeen, at the home of the Infantry;
My father is the father of all, Oh Mighty God,
Who guides us through uncertainty and pain
As my brothers and I march onto the fields of death.

Though driven by the spirit of past and the pace of the future
All of our endeavors are pursued with purpose;
A purpose known to only those who acknowledge the debt,
A debt that can never and will never be paid in full
Owed to the gallant, fallen sons of the Queen of Battle.

As a follower, I followed with confidence and determination
Being a servant of my people, I was their guardian from harm;
My trust in my leaders was deliberate and just,
For it is they who routed the path to victory
A victory earned by the sons of the Queen of Battle.

As a leader, I was able to separate passion from glory
Those serving under me, followed with trust and respect;
A trust never betrayed, respect never unearned,
I knew I must lead the way, but we all must open the door
As each of us becomes one, under the Queen of Battle.

Those of us not felled on the fields of death
Must approach a new horizon with self-imposed guilt;
As we reap the fruits of life, paid for from the blood,
Of our fallen brothers, who we reluctantly left behind
In the hands of God, and in the arms of the Queen of Battle.

THE SHIP

I have sat on the banks of the sea of life
While my ship sailed farther from shore;
The only ocean breeze I've felt
Is when they sent me off to war.

I've seen the lighthouse beacon flash
But its glow was much too weak;
I know a ship can bear no heading
When it has no point to seek.

The cliffs of life, I could never scale
To overlook the rugged sea;
And the deafening sound of silence
Captured my sense of being free.

I no longer walk those treacherous fields
Where bombs and bullets wail;
But the hands of time has beaten me
Diminishing the wind from my ship's sail.

The sea wall is my prison
Because if I should turn and go;
My ship of life may make it in
And I would never know.

THE GREAT AMERICAN WAY

The doer that doesn't is the winner that loses
No matter what goal one sets;
If the gambler gives one hundred-to-one odds
It's useless if nobody bets.

The fortunate take, the less fortunate must beg
Survival is the name of the game;
But those born with gold in hand
Keep the less fortunate economically lame.

The ticker tape crowd, it's said, is our backbone
And the rich get richer each day;
Our way of life keeps the poor, dirt poor
It's only the great American way.

Power may only be obtained by the using of lives
To produce an unsurpassable score;
They mass our youth ad expendable old
And march them off to war.

Wars are never fought by the ones who gain
Therefore, the gainers must stay;
But then again, why break with tradition
It's only the great American way.

DEAD SURVIVORS

Our rulers sent us off in force
To fight their filthy war;
We marched on to an un-drawn line
And were told to keep the score.

'Our cause is just', we were often told
'All the world shall view our might';
Our slaughtered brothers sprawled in pools of blood
Made us wonder who was right.

In a pathetic attempt to conceal their guilt
Our country displayed a wall of black;
Inscribed the names, over ten years late
Of those who never made it back.

Hurrah for those, the fallen brave
Death guaranteed your honor spared;
You didn't have to live the hurt and shame
Of fighting for those who never cared.

You lie in peace, so well deserved
Though the grave must be your bed;
You're still alive in all our hearts
It's we survivors who are really dead.

ONE BLACK ROSE

In a field of rye, where the heroes lie
From the bugle comes that mournful tone;
A mother so torn, who lost her first-born
Was standing there all alone.

A hand on her shoulder, was that of a soldier
From where he came nobody knows;
His uniform was old, his eyes stone cold
He handed her one black rose.

This flower brings you no joy, will not bring back your boy
But, it's meaning represents all of those dead;
Though the firing did cease, they cannot rest in peace
Their country shamed them on the fields where they bled.

There was blood on their gun, but no battle was won
The victors were those who stayed home;
The debt to them gone unpaid, their souls are waylaid
Like me, they shall eternally roam.

Just as she feared, the soldier disappeared
Leaving her with the memory of those;
Because of all those who don't care, she'll always be aware
Of the meaning of that one black rose.

FLIGHT 341

Crossing the great Pacific waters one last time
Might ships collide with the setting sun;
In the wake of tomorrow, there will always be sorrow
For those of us aboard Flight 341.

Soaring above the jungles of pain and despair
Heaven descends to meet the darkened sea;
Sounds of war fade away, except for those who stay
To pay for the cost of being free.

There was angry silence as we flew through the clouds
Knowing we fought a war that was never won;
To the guys left below, we hope they all know
Our prayers were with them on Flight 341.

No one would greet us with flowers and cheer
They cussed us and spit in our face;
With San Francisco in view, all of us knew
We'd be like lepers of the human race.

We were not villains of terror, nor demons from Hell
Just someone's American son;
We only hope and pray, that maybe some day
Homecomings will be different for Flight 341.

ANGELS ON THE BATTLEFIELD

There were angels on the battlefield
They, too, could feel our pain;
Ensuring no soldier walked alone
Through the jungles of bloody rain.

America finally built a Wall of Stone
With names embedded deep;
To commemorate the fallen brave
As they lie in eternal sleep.

There were angels on the battlefield
Where the jungle meets the sea;
I knew I would never have to die alone
They were always there with me.

Behind that Wall of Stone, many hide
They feel no guilt or shame;
If the Wall should last for evermore
Thank God, it will never bear their name.

There were angels on the battlefield
They knew we all were scared;
Many at home never wished us well
But, we knew the angels cared.

YOU MADE ME WHAT I'M NOT TODAY

You made me what I'm not today
No one can ever gain my trust;
Like a wingless bird in a fragile shell
I exist, only because I must.

I've felt the chill from the raging seas
Crawled on the treacherous jungle floor;
Jumped from the skies defying turbulent winds
Yet, you shamelessly asked of me more.

You made me what I'm not today
I was but a pawn on your table game;
As you bask and flourish on your bed of glory
I'll lie till death on my bed of shame.

Scoffed and berated by all of those
Demanding my blood with no offer of thanks;
Gave my youth, my heart, yes--even my soul
While serving in your honored ranks.

You made me what I'm not today
You're the seed that grew the vine;
As gluttons feast while they fare on lies
I lie in gutters filled with wine.

THE SILVER STAR

The years have quickly come and gone
Since Joe went off to war;
With glowing pride, no shame to hide
Proud of what he was fighting for.

His letters home told of all his dreams
And how his thoughts flowed to the past;
Now he must go, but they didn't know
This letter would be his last.

Joe would make just one more flight
Then they would place him in a long, black car;
A hero's rewards are few, but they all knew
The honor of his Silver Star.

The bugler blew the sound to TAPS
A Sadder sound is never heard;
Rifles fire in the sky to honor those who die
While under wing of the great American bird.

Joe's momma sits by an open window
Tears run down her cheeks as the children play;
As her mind grows dim, she thinks of him
Playing out there by the window each day.

On her dying bed, she whispered softly
To her loved ones who stood so near;
"When that Silver Star turns solid gold
My son, Joe, will reappear."

A VALLEY CALLED IA DRANG

In nineteen hundred sixty-five
The winds of war began to wail;
America's youth, never told the truth
As to why they were set to sail.

The First Air Cavalry got the call
When the bells of freedom rang;
From political greed, spawned the poison seed
Leading us to a valley called Ia Drang.

Our sky soldiers were baptized in this valley of blood
Satan's demons were manning the gate;
No one had the key, no one could be free
When political agendas consist of power and hate.

Many sat in judgment, reaping their rewards
While our soldiers were dying in vain;
There was never a doubt, any man would walk out
The same man that walked into Ia Drang.

This battle had taken over three hundred lives
The price of our victory was much too high;
So much pain and despair, so few even care
That our soldiers, for nothing, would die.

The war in Vietnam would last another ten years
A war where freedom's bell should have never rang;
Almost sixty thousand lives lost, a sorrowful cost
That all started in a valley called Ia Drang.

THE DARK SIDE OF NOW

Lady Liberty's torch grants freedom
To even those undeserving somehow;
With our blood we paid, through uncertain terms
While living the dark side of now.

Yesterday is a long past memory
A past now gone forever;
As we struggle through each coming day
Walking on the edge of never.

Tragedy has become more common place
In our world so marred with shame;
We count only our dollars, not our blessings
And use, in vain, God's name.

We let Satan present his torch of fire
Gluttons feast on red meat and wine;
The useless becoming more useless each day
As they form in the welfare line.

Liberty's torch lights all paths to freedom
To greed and filth we all must bow;
As we are condemned to be the damned
While living the dark side of now.

CHILDREN OF STONE

Beware of the children, the children of stone
With the absence of love and always alone;
They cast not a shadow, but only a mark
Their symbol of presence silhouetted by the dark.

A silence to ensure the victory from pain
Mournful screams within magnified by the rain;
The horror of life seemingly too great
While the reward of death often too late.

Beware of the children, the children of stone
They can never be free in life so alone;
Wrathful hearts with burdens so deep
Persistence of sorrow accompanies their sleep.

Mellow tones of the wind interrupted by lies
Bring echoes of thunder from nature's fierce cries;
Somber stares of the children awaiting their fate
Victims of life, the offspring of hate.

Beware of the children, the children of stone
Their bodies entombed in the ground so alone;
Bewilderment took over their minds while so young
The children of stone die off unsung.

THE SCRIPT'S FINAL PAGE

With graying hair and a wrinkled brow
I realize that yesterday is no part of now;
One must view life as a theatrical stage
Where the script is near written, except one final page.

Friends become fewer while the graveyards flourish
It seems death is a fuel that life needs to nourish;
Death in itself is not an evil tone
The evil is when one must die all alone.

I feel no serenity in the views I once cherished
Only the agony of truth that unity has perished;
The depth of one's thoughts becomes deeper with age
With their meaning all written on the script's final page.

The time that we borrow to keep up life's pace
Must all be repaid at the end of our race;
Life's not a gift, it's a chore we must heed
Our conscience must guide us until our soul's finally freed.

Most of us beg forgiveness for mistakes that we make
And feel fully justified when we wrongfully take;
Together we shall all meet at the center of stage
When the truth is all written on the script's final page.

THAT ONE FINAL DAY

Dreams seldom last beyond first light
Leaving the horrors of realism to pass in the night;
We focus on life as we know it today
Knowing we are all destined to that one final day.

Depth of one's vision rules all the late years
Defining all truths along with the fears;
We must brace to the wind while facing the rain
Then harness our thoughts into full refrain.

Time fades the sight as the mind grows less keen
Remembering less each day of the life we have seen;
There seems to be less faith when we kneel down to pray
As we drift to the downside of that one final day.

The progression of time is more difficult to endure
A once positive mind becomes less and less sure;
Days flash by without the freshness of youth
Only to collide with the harshness of truth.

We can never recapture the youth that we've spent
As our body gains age, a message is sent;
Both the rich and the poor shall wither away
Then we all become equals on that one final day.

OH WITHERED ROSE

A child of sorrow with deep set eyes
Kneeling by a granite marker stone;
Gazing at a single flower on the ground
Lying there all alone.

The child's tiny frame begins to fade
When the quarter moon appeared;
Descending stars helped light the field
As the child disappeared.

Withered rose, oh withered rose
Time has robbed you of your scent;
You and my Daddy had so much life
I wonder where it went.

Thunder roared from up above
A star bright sky turned solid black;
Then a timber fell from a lightning bolt
With a deathly frightening crack.

Seconds passed, then all was calm
It wasn't clear what had occurred;
There was silence in the still of night
When the child's fading voice was heard.

Withered rose, oh withered rose
You once graced my father's mound;
His body rots but his soul's now free
Of all sorrow above the ground.

HATRED IN FRIENDLY SKIES

There was a thunderous blast from above
In the land where freedom lies;
Poison rain fell, creating kitchens of hell
As hatred descended from friendly skies.

Sickening scents of ash and burning flesh
Lingers in the thickened air;
Embers violently burn, wherever you turn
Horror and devastation is everywhere.

Tears flow down the rescuers' cheeks
As they search and listen for human cries;
They, too, will die--only God knows why
When hatred descends from friendly skies.

All persons are free, once upon our shores
One can pursue any dream they choose;
The choices we make, others may try to take
Those who desire to see us lose.

The Eagle's feathers are ruffled but still will soar
Our grounds are bloody where Liberty lies;
With all of our might, we'll stand and fight
Against all hatred in friendly skies.

SEPTEMBER 11ᵀᴴ, TWO THOUSAND AND ONE

September 11, Two Thousand and One
Satan's disciples arrived straight from Hell;
Grievances unknown, terrorists' cowardice shown
As our New York skyline fell.

Cowards roam where cowards roam
Must we accept the scum of the earth?
Free to come in, murder thousands within
Those taught hatred from the day of their birth.

September 11, Two Thousand and One
Our Pentagon was attacked from the air;
Cowards' entry not denied, thus, many more died
The time has come to show that we care.

As cowards roam free, we all become victims
It's way past due that something be done;
Is Liberty's torch too bright? Something's not right
When the score is six thousand to none.

September 11, Two Thousand and One
The promise of more death was sealed;
Another jet seized in the sky, more people would die
Deliberately crashed in a Pennsylvania field.

Cowards are cowards, whomever they are
Makes no difference wherever they come from;
Must we now close our shores? Lock all our doors?
While those cowards beat on their native drums.

September 11, Two Thousand and One
A day America should never forget;
The Eagle shaken awake, for our country's sake
Make September 11th the day those cowards regret.

HEROES

Heroes don't usually come in bunches
But they sure did that day;
With one last breath, many met their death
All the rest stayed anyway.

From the depths of poverty to the height of wealth
Their views became much the same;
With death they flirt, they endure the hurt
From all walks of life they came.

Heroes don't usually come in bunches
Disaster brought them face to face;
Through all the madness, they'd share the sadness
Caused by scum of the human race.

God bless all those police and firefighters
Nurses, doctors, and all the rest;
Differences put aside, in respect for those who died
America saw its' people at their best.

Heroes don't usually come in bunches
This time that's how it was done;
Time may heal, but it will always be real
The events of September Eleven, Two Thousand and One.

OSAMA BIN LADEN

Osama Bin Laden, your secrets are known
You molest babies and camels until they are grown;
Long, dirty whiskers, you're ugly and stink
Sadam Hussein and you would look better in pink.

The ground which you walk is contaminated land
Your head stays buried in the Arabian sand;
Sadam Hussein of Iraq is your hero, I suppose
You probably pick boogers out of each others' nose.

Osama Bin Laden, you're scum of the earth
It's a shame your mother never gave birth;
You're supposed to be human, but you don't look the part
Means as a snake and smell like an outdated fart.

The fortune you have was amassed by others
Your followers are the offspring of unwed mothers;
You are widely known as a desert-fried fool
An Arabian land fill is all you're fit to rule.

Osama Bin Laden, there's something you need to know
The wart on your brain continues to grow;
Your lips will soon fall off the front of your face
And your testicles will be relocated in their place.

Your butt will be raised to the back of your neck
Allowing your followers' noses to easily intersect;
You are no doubt, the best known coward ever born
Who is soon to become just another broken thorn.

Osama Bin Laden, I bid you farewell
Even Satan may decline your presence in Hell;
Lives that you shattered will never be forgot
Humanity looks forward to the day that you rot.

THOSE HARBOR LIGHTS

God gave me vision, vision of day
Blurred and distorted by my life's oversights;
My destiny is now an un-plotted course
Away from those harbor lights.

In the sea of anger where ships collide
Life takes the form of one bitter storm;
From the endless depths, where boundaries lie
The fires of Satan are born.

There are no entries on my ship's manifest
The ship's hull, a huge empty core;
No spoken words could change the direction of sail
My ship has sailed too far from shore.

Cold, whistling winds, nature's angry response
To a life not lived by the rule;
Abuse of my time has banished all dreams
All that remains is the shell of a fool.

Oh, master of beacons, I bow before the mast
I face your tower that graces the sky;
Give me vision to focus on those harbor lights
Just one more time before I die.

BEYOND SHADOWS OF GRAY

Demeaning life in search of all the glitter and gold
Sleeping on beds where no man should stray;
A body so wrenched with pain from self abuse
Too weak to move beyond shadows of gray.

Cries of a child ring out in his mind
As the cold air cracks the skin on his face;
He was the child, whose cries he had heard
Whose youth disappeared without a trace.

There can be no fond memories in a life of despair
When one's youth is all wasted away;
The best you can hope for is an Angel of Grace
Who can lead you beyond shadows of gray.

The sting of cheap whiskey burns in his throat
As he tries to draw away all his grief;
Of all the bottles he drained, this was his last
The mercy of Heaven was to grant his relief.

A piercing pain in his side gave way to his soul
As he life started fading away;
An Angel of Grace finally set his soul free
Being lead beyond shadows of gray.

FINAL HOUR

She stood there in the silence of night
As a star streaked across Heaven's sky;
The fate of death took her only love
On a field where soldiers die.

No amount of courage could ease the pain
Only God would have that power;
There were no tears in her saddened eyes
As she approached her final hour.

Walking down through the scented fields
Where Nature's flower garden grows;
In her hand she grasped the stem
Of one pretty, yellow rose.

The winds now wail relentlessly
Across the lifeless field;
Their star of love shall now glow forever
Providing them both an eternal shield.

She knelt beside a mound of upturned earth
Upon it she place the flower;
Beside the rose laid her band of gold
This was now her final hour.

NO ONE SHOULD HAVE TO WALK THIS EARTH ALONE

There were no trophies on the mantle piece
No diplomas on the wall;
Some family members often wondered
Why he ever went to school at all.

The biting pain of being less
Than others wanted him to be;
Became a burden that he would bear
That those others failed to see.

No one should have to walk this earth alone
We all can't be the same;
Why must one have to die to show their worth
Being one's self should bear no shame.

His name was seldom mentioned by those he knew
Except when used for ridicule;
He found life's road was full of curves
But he had lived by the Golden Rule.

He died a hero on the battlefield
Saving lives he didn't even know;
Never turned his back on his fellow man
Maybe he can now rest where heroes go.

No one should have to walk this earth alone
On that darkened path he had traveled far;
That path now glows from Heaven's light
Given off by God's brightest star.

WE FOUGHT TOO

To the Veterans of the big wars
Labeled World War One and Two;
You all came back as heroes
And that, you all were due.

We know of the hardships you endured
And the losses you sustained;
The muddy fields that bogged you down
Especially when it rained.

The many months you got no mail
A hot meal you seldom had;
The air support that didn't come
When the weather had turned bad.

We're aware of the times you bowed your head
You would weep and say a prayer;
And often felt there was no God
Else he wouldn't have sent you there.

Your victories are justly recorded
From the Rock of the Marne down through Bastonge;
To the sands of Iwo Jima
Where our Marines had fought alone.

Then there was Normandy and Corregador
Where our paratroopers died in the air;
And the sailors on ships now deep beneath
On December 7th near Hawaii somewhere.

We heard about our airmen
Outnumbered ten to one;
Thanks to their guts and will to fight
For the battles they, too, had won.

Yes, we know about the millions
Who greeted you in New York that day;
When you came proudly marching home
You earned your right of way.

Your privileges were well deserved
Thank God, our nation thanked you well;
You didn't deserve to be subjected
To that damned Vietnam Hell.

To our Veterans of the Korean war
We also know of your deeds;
Of the many time you went without
When we couldn't fulfill your needs.

Yes, we know about your battles
In that "frozen chosen" land;
When the Chinese stormed you by the thousands
And you fought them hand-to-hand.

The infamous battle on Heartbreak Ridge
You made those bastards pay;
They hurt you bad and you suffered much
But, you became stronger every day.

We heard about other hills and ridges
Where your blood flowed down in streams;
And the landing you made at Inchon
That shattered many dreams.

Your war wasn't very popular
From the time it started until all through;
But, thank God, you still got thanked
And you marched home proudly, too.

You also earned your privileges
For heroically doing your job so well;
And you shouldn't have been subjected
To that damned Vietnam Hell.

Then it came our time to go
Like you, we joined the ranks;
We loaded up our Howitzers
And fueled up all the tanks.

We were loaded aboard the ships and planes
Southeast Asia was to be our stage;
But, we weren't there very long at all
When Americans started the anti-Vietnam rage.

They called us every filthy name
And paid visits to Hanoi town;
Communists were told how wrong we were
As the bullets cut our soldiers down.

Our war lingered about ten years
And finally told to crawl away;
For almost the sixty thousand who gave their lives
I wonder what they'd have to say.

We of Vietnam came straggling home
Without honor, glory, or fame;
The fat from war on "Capitol Hill"
Gave us the privilege of the shame.

We weren't aware of the drugs we used
But, according to the media, it must be true;
Because our country damned us good
When the fighting was finally through.

The troops who fought in Vietnam
Didn't return to the sound of brass;
As we shed our country's uniforms
We were classified "Citizen--Second Class."

We knew better than to expect your thanks
Being aware of your feelings before;
Please just forget we ever were
And don't shame us any more.

We love this country and respect its laws
And know the meaning of the Liberty Bell;
But, don't ever ask us to go again
To another damned Vietnam Hell.

BUBBA JOE'S GONE A HUNTIN'

Bubba Joe McCarley, an ole' Alabama boy
Was raised on the pickins of the land;
Made him mad as Hell when the Trade Center fell
He's going after those mean, little suckers in the sand.

He don't much cotton to the way they dress
Got those diapers wrapped around their head;
And their women folk must be ugly as sin
If their face ain't covered, they're dead.

Bubba Joe's going a huntin' fer Arabs in the sand
Bet he kills him a million or so;
Reckon when he gets his gun, he'll have 'em on the run
Be like shootin' a bunch of ducks in a row.

Thar goes Bubba Joe McCarley, lookin' ever so fine
Yonder way just a struttin' his stuff;
He's like an Airborne Ranger, lookin' for danger
That big hillbilly sure is tough.

Momma kissed him goodbye, Pappa shook his hand
The ole' hound dog licked his face;
Aunt Gracie a prayin', her boney knees a swayin'
And Preacher John singin', "Amazin' Grace."

Bubba Joe's going a huntin' fer Arabs in the sand
All dressed up in his BDUs;
Got him an M-16 and a Rocket Launch Machine
Singin' "Ole Bin Ladin Gonna Have the Blues."

Go get 'em, Bubba Joe, make us ever so proud
Make 'em rot under that Arabian sun;
They not very nice, make 'em pay the price
Shoot 'em with your big ole' Army gun.

Ya just gotta envy that big ole' fool
He's Alabama's pride and joy;
His brain may be a bit small, but he answered the call
Bubba Joe is our all-American boy.

Bubba Joe's going a huntin' for Arabs in the sand
Got his M-16 gun on cruise;
With a big, goofy grin, Bubba Joe's out to win
Osama and the Taliban are a gonna lose!

United States of America

United We Stand!

www.ingramcontent.com/pod-product-compliance
Lightning Source LLC
Chambersburg PA
CBHW041552220426
43666CB00002B/46